EDIBLE
CITY

EDIBLE CITY

MUSEUM OF HISTORY & INDUSTRY | REBEKAH DENN

lairdnorton
WEALTH MANAGEMENT

Published in conjunction with the exhibit *Edible City: A Delicious Journey* organized by the Museum of History & Industry (MOHAI), November 2016–September 2017.

This publication was made possible by Laird Norton Wealth Management. The exhibit *Edible City: A Delicious Journey* is presented by ✈ *BOEING*

Additional support provided by Oxbow Farm & Conservation Center, PCC Natural Markets, The Julia Child Foundation for Gastronomy and the Culinary Arts, Tulalip Tribes, 4Culture, Mike Repass, and Edward and Marylyn Gregory.

ISBN: 978-0-692-74040-8

Design: Beth Koutsky
Copy editor/proofreader: Carrie Wicks
Publication coordinator: Kate Fernandez

Color and print management by iocolor, Seattle
Printed in China at Artron Color Printing Ltd.

MUSEUM OF HISTORY & INDUSTRY

860 Terry Avenue | Seattle, WA 98109 | MOHAI.org

CONTENTS

People's Pantry
Stories scattered throughout about people who
have shaped Seattle's food industry.

FOREWORD

Leonard Garfield

⬤▬▬

How many communities can trace their history to the simple ingredient of clam nectar?

In 1851, members of the Duwamish Tribe, first peoples of Seattle, offered nutritious clam nectar to the earliest American pioneers at Alki Point, helping those settlers survive and ultimately thrive in their new home. Thus began a long relationship between newcomers and those who always made Seattle home— and a strong connection between the food we eat and the place where we live.

Nearly two centuries later, we are still a region whose culinary traditions, like its people, are distinguished by the confluence of cultures, the wise use of natural resources, and the willingness (and oftentimes necessity) to try something new. *Edible City* celebrates that rich heritage, saluting the roots of a unique food culture while heralding the new faces and new techniques that are forever reinventing our city.

Edible City is a companion book to the Museum of History & Industry (MOHAI) exhibit on display in the Walker Gallery from November 2016 to September 2017. This book, the exhibit, and the programs that accompany it benefited from the remarkable insights of Rebekah Denn, who served as both author and curator; the community advisory committee that guided the project; MOHAI's exceptional staff and Board of Trustees; and the many individuals whose stories, artifacts, and generosity helped bring this delicious dinner to life.

I am especially honored to salute Laird Norton Wealth Management as lead *Edible City* book sponsor and am grateful for the generous support of The Boeing Company, Mike Repass, Tom Alberg and Judi Beck, and Oxbow Farm & Conservation Center, which was essential to the success of the *Edible City* exhibit.

It's been a long time since clam nectar was our beverage of choice, but Seattle is still a city with a distinctive food culture. MOHAI is pleased to share that complex and unfolding story in these pages. Dig in and enjoy!

INTRODUCTION

Nancy Leson

As a Seattle restaurant critic and food writer for nearly a quarter century, I've chronicled the rise of our "edible" city as a home for enthusiastic food lovers. As a curious and omnivorous cook, I've been aware of its abundance even longer.

Here in Seattle, I've learned to anticipate the gentle pop of an oyster knife as it exposes a briny bivalve; the soundtrack of buskers, fishmongers, and produce purveyors as I make my way through Pike Place Market; and the sight of a crab pot dancing with Dungeness pulled from the depths of Puget Sound.

Native born or newcomer, we have so much to celebrate.

With Pacific Northwest pride we share our home-smoked salmon and our homegrown apples, the miracle of chanterelle mushrooms and the magic of fiddlehead ferns. We trade pints of huckleberries for pints of homemade beer, and Rainier cherries for heirloom seedpods, passed on from pioneers.

Together, we travel the world without a passport in the well-stocked aisles of gargantuan Asian supermarkets, and in the comforting confines of Szechuan bistros and Vietnamese cafes. We're as adept at pickling Yakima asparagus as we are Korean kimchi, and as likely to bring sushi to our potlucks as strawberry shortcake.

The Coastal Salish could not have imagined that someday their native clams would find company steamed with Spanish chorizo or Thai curry, nor that a time would come when their plentiful Chinook salmon—sauced with spring nettles—would fetch forty dollars per precious fillet.

In Seattle, we appreciate our homegrown restaurants whether they are classic or contemporary, haute or hole-in-the-wall. Our diverse neighborhoods support talented chefs and charismatic restaurateurs who encourage us to celebrate all that's local, seasonal, and sustainable.

Today, Seattle sprouts skyscrapers and innovative industries at breakneck speed. Yet like those who lived on this land before us, we soothe our bodies and souls knowing that despite the modern momentum, we can still turn to our mountains and forests, lakes and rivers, gardens and orchards, and to one another, and rejoice in our region's bounty.

Ours are delicious riches, defined by the geography and history acknowledged in the coming pages by author Rebekah Denn and the Museum of History & Industry: proof positive that, when it comes to our Emerald City, there truly is no place like home.

Chapter 1.

MORE THAN A MEAL

In Seattle, food has always meant more than a meal.

Our journey from the earliest oyster middens to the modern four-star restaurants is a reflection of our geography, our history, and our people.

Location is everything: Seattle is close to fishing and shellfish harvesting grounds, close to fertile farmland and foraging areas. Institutions dedicated to food are concentrated in our region, from the agricultural research labs at Washington State University to the fishing fleet headquartered here and the factories processing their catches.

Diversity is key to our success: throughout generations, the city has attracted immigrants who bring their own culinary traditions and skills, with a lively population of young, creative, and international residents hungry for familiar flavors. Seattle's resources and natural beauty made it a place where, even during tough times, people didn't want to leave.

Here, a commitment to homegrown foods went well beyond World War II Victory Gardens. A critical mass of idealists interested in self-sufficiency and fresh ingredients consistently gained support from businesses and municipalities, making for a collaborative culture embracing robust food co-ops and a closely connected network of farmers and chefs.

Size also matters: Seattle is large enough to accommodate new breakthroughs, yet still small enough to foster a sense of community.

LEFT Fishing boats moored at Fishermen's Terminal in 1936. The terminal reminds Seattleites where our food comes from; it's still a working dock and home to the North Pacific Fishing Fleet.

PREVIOUS PAGE London Plane, one of an influx of restaurants making historic Pioneer Square once again a central place to eat.

Tea and . . . Fry Bread?

Who would expect a tea party as a way to promote tribal traditions? In Seattle's case, it would be Cecile Hansen, chairwoman of the Duwamish Tribe and direct descendent of Princess Angeline, daughter of Chief Seattle. Several years ago, to encourage the community to visit the Duwamish Longhouse, Hansen began holding a free annual Princess Angeline's Tea Party. Serving sweets and savories, this April tradition combines favorites old and new: salmon, of course, and Native teas as well as English imports, finger sandwiches as well as occasional fry bread. Staple Duwamish foods often came from fishing, hunting, and foraging.

Cecile Hansen preparing fry bread.

ABOVE The Yesler Mill Cookhouse on First Avenue South, built in 1852, served as the city's first restaurant as well as a center of civic life.

OPPOSITE The waters of Puget Sound were home to an abundance of salmon and salmon fishermen. In this circa 1910 photo, visitors watch tons of live salmon being dumped from a trap into a barge in northern Puget Sound.

The city has become one of the country's top places to eat and innovate. And while it took more than a century to establish a definable Seattle cuisine, its raw ingredients were here all along.

Seattle's geography had traditionally allowed fishermen, foragers, and farmers to feed themselves. Its waterways and shores were rich Native harvesting grounds for every sort of wild food, from salmon to smelt. Tribal members dug wapato bulbs and picked serviceberries, little known today beyond private tribal events or educational presentations. They also foraged delicacies as trendy on modern restaurant plates as blackcap raspberries and miner's lettuce.

As for dining out, there have been eateries in Seattle just about as long as there have been workers here to support them. The cedar-plank Yesler's Cookhouse, built in 1852, is credited as the original Seattle restaurant— as well as its first civic center, courthouse, general hangout, and jail. It soon had competitors, and by 1865, weekly meals could be procured at comparably more refined institutions such as the Occidental Hotel.

By the 1880s there was a downtown spate of more than a dozen restaurants, including an all-night lunch counter. These were devastated by the Great Seattle Fire of 1889—but the city and its restaurants were quickly rebuilt. That resurrection sparked new landmarks like the brick building in Pioneer Square that still houses the Merchants Cafe.

Still Nutty

Even peanut butter was once considered a local food. Adams Peanut Butter, now owned by Smucker's, was founded in 1916 by Tacoma football coach Rex Adams, who took pride in a product so fresh it was still warm when delivered to stores. The "Sunny Jim" peanut butter once popular throughout the West Coast was founded in Seattle by Germanus Wilhelm Firnstahl, who bought his first peanut roaster in 1921 and sold his goods at Pike Place Market. The smiling boy's face on the Sunny Jim logo and Georgetown factory was modeled after Firnstahl's son.

Today there's a local brand again, CB's Nuts in Kitsap County, where owners Clark and Tami Bowen roast, grind, and package US-grown nuts. Serendipitously, they bought and refurbished one of the original Adams roasters to do so. The one-ton machine roasts just ninety-five pounds of in-shell peanuts at a time, a fraction of the tons handled by modern industrial outfits. "It's a slower pace, that's for sure," Clark said, but he loves both its history and craft. "The product it makes is second to none."

Sunny Jim peanut butter label.

Hopeful miners in the Klondike Gold Rush boosted business. Bivalve purveyors arose, among them the Haines Oyster House, founded by a Civil War veteran, credited as the first to serve Pacific oysters. G.O. Guy, one of a handful of druggists claiming credit for inventing the ice-cream soda, established a drugstore at Second and Yesler in 1892 after his original shop was burned in the fire. It operated twenty-four hours a day for decades, growing into a citywide chain. Chauncey Wright of the Seattle Restaurant Company was already dubbed a dining pioneer by the *Seattle Daily Times* in 1911. The paper noted that, starting with his work in his father's Seattle restaurant thirty years earlier, "there had always been that name of Wright on a restaurant window in this city."[1] Always crowded Manca's, founded in 1899, was credited with inventing Dutch Baby pancakes, while Maison Blanc, a landmark from 1916 to 1960, advertised "aristocratic" meals from around the world "at a democratic price."

From its earliest days onward, the twists and turns of the city's foodways have reflected those of its residents, as diverse as the "fine new lutefisk" advertised at the Westlake Market in 1912[2] and the Ethiopian restaurants first opened by UW students in 1982.

ABOVE Two 1950s examples of canned salmon brands distributed by Seattle companies. Modern Seattle may be better known for aerospace and computer technology, but it is still home to some of the country's largest seafood distributors. (One of them, Ocean Beauty, had its roots in the 1910 Washington Fish and Oyster Company on Seattle's waterfront, while Trident Seafoods was founded here in 1961.)

RIGHT Many Asian immigrants in King County in the early twentieth century were farmers. In this photo, taken in the Seattle area around 1919, a strawberry picker displays a flat of berries. Washington currently produces about 1 percent of the nation's strawberries, intensely flavored varieties that are often too fragile to travel.

Lasting Flavors

A Seattle food tour would have looked very different a few generations in the past. A handful of stops, though, would be as familiar to our grandparents as they are to us.

Tim Louie, proprietor of the Tsue Chong factory in Seattle's Chinatown-International District once told a reporter he had been very fortunate. In truth, he's the one, along with generations of his family members, who have been key in spreading good fortunes. The factory, which produces fortune cookies and a wide variety of Asian noodles, was founded in 1917 by his great-grandfather, Gar Hip Louie, an immigrant from China's Guangdong province. The company's Rose Brand noodles are known around the Northwest, served in countless restaurants, and sold to customers at the walk-in factory store. Bags of "unfortunate" factory-reject cookies are still the freshest, crispiest versions you might have the good luck to nibble.

As Italian families came to Seattle, so did their imports. Olive oil was the specialty of two major companies—Merlino, established in 1900 as Angelo Merlino & Sons, and A. Magnano & Sons, founded by Antonio Magnano in 1903. Their specialty was new to many Seattle consumers. Magnano, advertising "The Golden Oil of the Riviera"[3] around a century ago, suggested consuming two tablespoons daily to ensure "health and a fine complexion." The Merlino company issued a cookbook on the oil's use. Both companies are thriving today: Magnano's distribution and importing business is now the Napoleon Co., run by the family's fourth generation. Merlino Foods is owned by the Biesold family and still supplies many of the city's best restaurants. Angelo Merlino's

grandson, Armandino Batali, created the Salumi meat company, a modern legend. Great-grandson Mario Batali has his own olive oil brand, though that's the least of his fame.

Maneki—founded around 1904 in the Japantown neighborhood that flourished in the late nineteenth century and early twentieth century—is celebrated in Seattle for its Japanese comfort food and sushi, and as one of "America's Classics" by the James Beard Foundation. Takeo Miki, a future prime minister of Japan, washed dishes there. Mark Tobey, a founder of the Northwest School of painting, traded artwork for its food. Relocated to a second Japantown location after the internment of Japanese residents during World War II, Maneki remains a modern mainstay under the care of longtime owner Jeanne Nakayama.

As an adult he was the "jester of jerky."[4] As the son of Italian immigrants, growing up in "Garlic Gulch," Art Oberto was far from carefree. At age sixteen, after his father's death in 1943, he took over the family specialty meats business, biking from West Seattle High School to handle his new responsibilities. Working with his mother, he turned the business into a successful sausage factory and later an innovator of packaged beef jerky. The product became a huge success, and Oberto became a civic symbol with his "Oh Boy!" company slogan, his hydroplane sponsorships, and his Lincoln Town Car "jerky mobile." Nearly a century old, the company is still family owned.

William Gross (sometimes spelled "Grose"), an early leader in California's black community, saved money working for years in Seattle restaurants before opening his hospitable Our House restaurant in 1876 at First Avenue and what is now Yesler Way. Gross was known for generously feeding newcomers down on their luck, including future industrialist and Seattle mayor Robert Moran, who was treated to a big serving of pancakes, sausages, and coffee after arriving in Seattle as a hungry, broke teen. "Come back and pay me when you get work," Gross told Moran and many others. Our House was destroyed in Seattle's Great Fire of 1889; Gross went on to other successful businesses and was the anchor of what became Seattle's first African American neighborhood in the East Madison neighborhood.

While the original Dutch Baby recipe invented by Manca's Cafe is a secret, a version printed by *Sunset* magazine became one of its most popular recipes ever. This version is by Sharon Kramis, a founding member of Seattle's chapter of Les Dames d'Escoffier, and her daughter, food consultant and stylist Julie Kramis Hearne.

Dutch Baby

Makes 2 servings

2 tablespoons butter
4 extra-large eggs
⅔ cup all-purpose flour
⅔ cup whole milk

TOPPING
2 tablespoons butter, melted
Juice of 1 lemon
½ cup powdered sugar

Preheat oven to 425 degrees F.

To prepare the Dutch Baby, melt the butter in a 12-inch cast-iron skillet over low heat. Mix the eggs, flour, and milk in a blender on medium speed until just blended, 5 to 10 seconds. Pour the batter into the skillet with the melted butter.

Place the skillet in the oven and bake until the top puffs up and is lightly golden, about 25 minutes.

When the Dutch Baby is done, drizzle the melted butter over the top, and then sprinkle with the lemon juice and dust with the powdered sugar. Cut into six wedges and serve immediately.

ABOVE Manca's, credited with the invention of puffy Dutch Baby pancakes, opened before the turn of the century at Second Avenue and Cherry Street, then served generations of downtown workers and families during "banking hours" at 108 Columbia Street before the building was razed in 1955.

Chapter 2

LANDMARKS, LOST AND LASTING

Today, no sojourn to Seattle is considered complete without a visit to Pike Place Market. In 1907, it was a deeply practical innovation to ensure public access to produce.

Seattle's population was growing and food prices were soaring. Middlemen gouged both farmers and shoppers, spiking the cost of even the humblest onion.

Enter city councilman Thomas P. Revelle, who learned the city had actually authorized the creation of a public market just over a decade earlier. He introduced an ordinance in 1907 designating Pike Place as its location.

"It is now up to the public,"[5] directed the *Seattle Times*, urging customers to show up for opening day. And what a day it was. Amid fears of squabbles and sabotage, only a handful of farmers appeared. Customers swarmed the first to arrive, H.O. Blanchard, cheering as he approached with a load of vegetables. Every cart sold out by 11:00 a.m.

Market expansions followed almost immediately, some fueled by city funds, but most by businessmen.

Real estate developer Frank Goodwin, who made his fortune in the Klondike and "knew a gold mine when he saw one,"[6] owned some neighboring properties and promptly purchased more. By 1917, the Pike Place Market included a permanent arcade, a Sanitary Public Market (it banned horses), the Corner Market Building, the four-story main addition, and the Economy Market Building.

LEFT Ignore the clothing styles and vintage cars, and Pike Place Market stalls look about the same today as they did in historic photos. In this 1941 image, a vegetable vendor at Stall 82 shows off his crop of Bermuda onions.

UPPER An annual Sunday School picnic (most likely at Woodland Park) was a more formal event in 1917.

LOWER Many Italian immigrant families operated "truck farms" in south Seattle where produce was grown and trucked to market. Giuseppe "Joe" Desimone was a farming legend in the neighborhood. Eventually, by 1941, he owned Pike Place Market's main arcade. Now the Market is run by the nonprofit Pike Place Market Preservation & Development Authority chartered by the city.

The early years saw the debut of now-familiar names and debates. Squabbles over who was a "genuine farmer" rather than a reseller arose. The Three Girls Bakery introduced the city's first automatic donut caster in 1917, spellbinding children back then as the modern Daily Dozen Doughnut Company does today. Grocery owner Angelina Mustello welcomed bread deliveries in 1928 from a young Italian immigrant, Pete DeLaurenti, who later married her daughter Mamie. Their successor business, Pete's Italian Grocery, was a landmark for fine imported foods and evolved into today's DeLaurenti—at the Market's front door. The Market was also, if not equal opportunity, at least a place where different cultures and ethnicities mixed. Sephardic Jews were among the earliest vendors, joined by Japanese farmers and Greek restaurant owners.

Pike Place Market was far from the only culinary center, even in its early days.

Italian families established long-lived landmarks, especially in the "Garlic Gulch" of south Seattle. The eponymous family bakery opened by Mario Borrachini in 1923 is still going strong.

Elegant department store tearooms weren't out of the ordinary when Frederick & Nelson opened its version in its 1918 headquarters at Fifth and Pine. It became the stuff of sweet legend when, historian Robert Spector says, candy-kitchen head Ray Alden developed a Frango mint "meltaway" chocolate in 1927. The candy became synonymous with Seattle, even after Chicago's Marshall Field's stores began selling them in 1929. Spector says the secret recipe called for "cocoa beans from the African coast or South America, triple-distilled oil of Oregon peppermint and 40 percent butter."[7]

It seems fitting that the icon that survives almost unchanged is Ivar's, brainchild of engaging entrepreneur Ivar Haglund.

That larger-than-life showman, folk singer, and brilliant publicist backed a fish-and-chips restaurant in 1938, and later launched his Acres of Clams in 1946, credited as having Seattle's first kids' menu and amusements.

UPPER A woman working in the extracts department at Crescent Manufacturing Company, circa 1927. Founded in 1883 as Larsen Extract Company, Crescent manufactured some seventy-five different extracts by the early twentieth century, including Mapleine, a popular maple flavoring that was–back then–a household name.

LOWER Brothers Nick and Pat Vacca in 1940 working in their vegetable farm on the hillside above Sick's Stadium. When people discovered they could see games from the Vacca farm rather than pay the stadium admission, the hillside got the nickname Tightwad Hill.

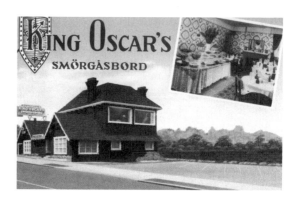

He expanded into fancier outlets like the Native-inspired Salmon House in 1969 and more casual ones like a fast-food chain.

Duwamish lore has it that tribal members taught settlers to nourish their babies on clam nectar. A half century later, Haglund advertised his "ever-rejuvenating clam nectar" as a mock aphrodisiac. No more than three cups would be served to any married man, he joked, "without written permission of his wife."

In Haglund's obituary, the *Seattle Times* summed up how he became an icon: "His relaxed philosophy, his generosity, his phenomenal business success, his intrigue with our past: these were qualities in which old Seattle instinctively saw itself."[8]

Others missed that iconic status.

In the 1920s and '30s the name Clare Colegrove was "associated with good eating in Seattle,"[9] with alliterative eateries like the Purple Pup. Walter Clark, known as the dean of Seattle restaurateurs, owned an astonishing fifty-five restaurants between 1930 and 1970 (including the iconic Twin T-P's), according to old-Seattle expert Clark Humphrey. A critic[10] once wrote that it was unlikely anyone in Seattle had not heard of Clark's restaurants. A few decades later, it was unlikely that anyone had.

Ironically, the beacon that made more of a lasting mark was not known for either fine fare or fancy decor. What it lacked in elegance it made up in heart and inclusiveness—because, as its slogan said: "All roads lead to the Dog House."

The saying was literal in the 1930s when Bob Murray strategically located his diner on "the best short block available"[11] at the southern end of the Aurora Speedway. (It moved to Seventh and Bell after traffic patterns changed with the opening of the Battery Street Tunnel.) The twenty-four-hour Dog House was "a restaurant for ordinary people,"[12] where waitresses took no guff, an organist played sing-alongs in the bar, and the rib-eye steak

UPPER King Oscar's Smorgasbord (c. 1950) on Aurora Avenue North, advertising "the true Scandinavian Smorgasbord as enjoyed in the land of the Vikings," was also known for its Swedish pancakes. Nordic fare isn't as common in twenty-first-century Seattle, but the Swedish Cultural Center still serves pancakes on the first Sunday of every month.

LOWER Laurie Gulbransen was a server when the Dog House opened in 1934, and the owner when it closed in 1994. The twenty-four-hour diner was a symbol of simpler, more down-to-earth days in Seattle.

OPPOSITE The iconic Twin T-P's restaurant was one of dozens of eateries owned by Walter Clark, serving family meals at reasonable prices. The eye-catching structure, which opened in 1937 on Aurora Avenue, was part of a trend of restaurant and hotel owners trying to capture the attention of drivers in a newly mobile community.

Known as the man who pioneered fast-food chains in Seattle, **Gill Centioli** and wife Alma founded Gil's Drive-In hamburgers in 1953 and went on to become one of the first franchisers for Kentucky Fried Chicken. Food was in the family: daughter **Dorene Centioli-McTigue** founded the Pagliacci Pizza Co., and son **Gerard** is a powerhouse of the restaurant business nationwide, including bringing the first Krispy Kreme franchises to Washington.

In 1954, **Dick Spady** cofounded Dick's Drive-In, claimed as the state's oldest continually operating fast-food restaurant. A stop by Dick's became a Seattle ritual for generations. The small chain is famed for inexpensive hamburgers and fries and shakes, served fast, but also for treating employees right.

came with the disclaimer that tenderness was not guaranteed. Sportswriters and sports stars might eat in adjoining booths, as did prostitutes and prosecutors. When the final last call came in 1994, spurred by changing tastes and dining habits, it was a dividing line between old Seattle and new. It had been that rare place, as the owner once told a reporter, where "we accept anybody and everybody, just like America does."[13]

Sadly, Seattle hasn't always lived up to that promise of acceptance.

Japanese farmers, who produced an estimated 75 percent of all produce sold in the Seattle area in the 1930s, comprised as many as half of Pike Place Market's five hundred stands before their forced relocation to internment camps under President Franklin Roosevelt's Executive Order 9066.

Just 196 stalls remained in 1942, despite the supposed benefits of an "all-American" white farmers' row. Berry farms on Bainbridge and Vashon Islands went untended, as did vegetable fields. Some said Pike Place Market was never the same—and in its ethnic makeup, it certainly was not.

Despite hardships and injustice, the wartime years also brought new energy to the growing city, which had seen a big population bump from

ABOVE For decades, Pete DeLaurenti was a legend of Pike Place Market. The shop that bears his name is still known for specialty foods.

OPPOSITE In this 1942 photo, the US Army removed more than two hundred Japanese American residents, including many farmers, from their homes and businesses on Bainbridge Island.

the manufacturing and engineering demands placed on Boeing. A better-traveled, better-educated workforce began a push for better dining.

A big boost came from the ability to drink while dining out. While Prohibition had been repealed in 1933, restaurants still hadn't been allowed to serve hard liquor by the drink. Once laws were updated in the 1940s, restaurants could do so if a large enough percentage of their revenues came from food rather than booze. That incentive for pricier fare set the industry "on fire," one business leader said.[14]

The first to benefit was Canlis, claiming to be Seattle's first restaurant with a liquor license. Probably no restaurant has evolved along with the city as much as it has.

When it debuted in 1950 as the Canlis Broiler, charcoal broilers were fashionable establishments and perfectionist founder Peter Canlis was already "internationally famous," for his eatery in Honolulu.[15] From opening day, valet Dick Sprinkle parked cars and retrieved them without ever requiring a ticket to match diner with vehicle. Canlis was the de rigueur stop for kings and kingpins. John Wayne favored it, battling the owner for the prime Table #1 with its telephone. The Canlis menu was innovative for its time, which meant mahimahi flown in from Hawaii and baked potatoes loaded with toppings.

Canlis offered a rare bit of glamour in unpretentious Seattle, still shaking off its old reputation as one of the worst restaurant cities in America.

When preservationist Bill Speidel Jr. told a friend in the 1950s that he was writing a book on Seattle's fine eateries, the humorist described the reply as "Oh, yeah? Well, it'll have to be a mighty thin book."[16]

Slowly, though, the numbers grew.

The elegant Cloud Room at the Camlin Hotel (which lays a competing claim to that first liquor license) began serving in 1949. Ruby Chow,

ABOVE Debonair restaurateur Peter Canlis set out to impress with a modernist Roland Terry building overlooking Lake Union. And so he did, dressing his waitresses in Japanese kimonos (pictured here in 1958) and his dining room with flowers "flown in daily" from the islands. While the kimono dress code has long been retired, Peter's grandsons more recently brought in dancers from Pacific Northwest Ballet to train the staff in light-footed service.

Keep Clam and Carry On

How zany were the exploits of Ivar's founder Ivar Haglund? Take this true-false test (answers at bottom).

1. He opened Seattle's first aquarium.

2. A talented musician, his famous "Acres of Clams" slogan came from a song that he was personally taught by Pete Seeger and Woody Guthrie.

3. He once pushed a seal in a baby carriage to see Santa at Frederick & Nelson's.

4. He once arranged for a heavyweight boxer to wrestle an octopus in a tank. The Humane Society complained, but it turned out later the octopus was already dead.

5. He played the role of "First Mate Salty" on a children's TV show.

6. A drive-in Ivar's once offered Chinese and Mexican food as well as seafood.

7. Outraged by a postage stamp featuring a sardine, Ivar once printed his own clam stamps. The feds ordered them destroyed.

8. Ivar once purchased the Smith Tower and flew a giant salmon wind sock from its flagpole.

Answers: All true! Three cups of clam nectar for you if you guessed them right.

A messy syrup spill from a tank car provided the perfect opportunity for media-savvy restaurateur Ivar Haglund.

Source: *Ivar: The Life and Times of Ivar Haglund* by Dave Stephens.

the matriarch of Seattle's Chinese American community for decades, opened the relatively upscale Ruby Chow's in 1948, which historian Walt Crowley described as "the Democratic party clubhouse"[17] for King County. Its very location made a statement; the First Hill gathering place was the city's first Chinese restaurant outside of its Chinatown.

For home cooks, Asian ingredients were also becoming more broadly available thanks to Fujimatsu Moriguchi. In 1928 he established a business selling fish cakes and Japanese ingredients to laborers in Tacoma. He was imprisoned in the Tule Lake internment camp during the war, but "whatever his bitter feelings and doubts,"[18] a *Seattle Times* columnist once wrote, he returned in 1946 and sunk $400 into a flagship Seattle Uwajimaya store, named for his hometown of Uwajima.

Then, a chance decision helped tip Seattle's dining scene into enviable elegance.

ABOVE Ruby Chow in the kitchen, circa 1960. A trailblazer from her popular restaurant to her political career, the King County councilwoman was known for "roast duck diplomacy." The name comes from the dish she brought to Senator Warren Magnuson when successfully lobbying to keep a federal prison out of Chinatown.

Tacoma native Victor Rosellini had worked in San Francisco for years and expected to open his own Italian restaurant there. But Seattle, he decided, was the true niche for his vision. When he opened Rosellini's 610 in 1950, its sophistication, along with his own warm personality and savvy, made it the place to be. In an astonishing decision at the time, he didn't install a lunch counter, but presented a communal roundtable instead. The 610 became home to a bipartisan group of movers and shakers, political gatherings and anniversary dinners, chateaubriand and champagne. His next outpost, the elegant Rosellini's Four-10, won similar acclaim.

It's become "an article of faith" one writer said in later years,[19] that Rosellini, along with Canlis and a few others such as El Gaucho, spurred a revolution in the Seattle restaurant business. Among Rosellini's contributions: white linen tablecloths, cut flowers, numbered wine lists—and customer care that made guests feel "very very important, no matter what their station in life."

LEFT Visitors to the Country Inn roadhouse in Georgetown (c. 1914) could take a carriage or streetcar right to the door, or opt for the "Automobile Entrance." The tavern became the Carleton Avenue Grocery, a corner grocery that's still in business and advertised as the oldest in the city.

RIGHT Victor Rosellini beams over his guests at his Four-10 Restaurant at 410 University Street in 1959. Retired restaurant critic John Hinterberger once said that when he was in graduate school the Four-10 "was the place I saved up my money and went to once a year."

Kurt Beecher Dammeier has led a charge to make Washington cheeses as successful as Washington wines. Dammeier's own Beecher's Handmade Cheese in Pike Place Market has won top national awards and wows Market visitors with a close-up view of cheesemakers at work.

Beecher's World's Best Mac and Cheese

Serves 4 as a side dish

6 ounces penne pasta
2 cups Beecher's Flagship Cheese Sauce (recipe follows)
1 ounce cheddar, grated (¼ cup)
1 ounce Gruyère cheese, grated (¼ cup)
¼ to ½ teaspoon chipotle chile powder

Preheat oven to 350 degrees F.

Oil or butter an 8-inch baking dish.

Cook the penne 2 minutes less than package directions.
(It will finish cooking in the oven.) Rinse pasta in cold water and set aside.

Combine cooked pasta and Flagship Sauce in a medium bowl and mix carefully but thoroughly. Scrape the pasta into the prepared baking dish. Sprinkle the top with the cheeses and then the chile powder. Bake, uncovered, for 20 minutes. Let sit for 5 minutes before serving.

Note: If you double the recipe to make a main dish, bake in a 9-by-13-inch pan for 30 minutes.

BEECHER'S FLAGSHIP CHEESE SAUCE

Makes about 4 cups, enough for a double batch

¼ cup (½ stick) unsalted butter
⅓ cup all-purpose flour
3 cups milk
14 ounces semihard cheese, such as Beecher's Flagship, grated (about 3½ cups)
2 ounces grated semisoft cheese, such as Beecher's Just Jack
½ teaspoon kosher salt
¼ to ½ teaspoon chipotle chile powder
⅛ teaspoon garlic powder

Melt the butter in a heavy-bottom saucepan over medium heat, and whisk in the flour. Continue whisking and cooking for 2 minutes. Slowly add the milk, whisking constantly. Cook until the sauce thickens, about 10 minutes, stirring frequently. Remove from the heat. Add the cheese, salt, chile powder, and garlic powder. Stir until the cheese is melted and all ingredients are incorporated, about 3 minutes. Use immediately, or refrigerate for up to 3 days.

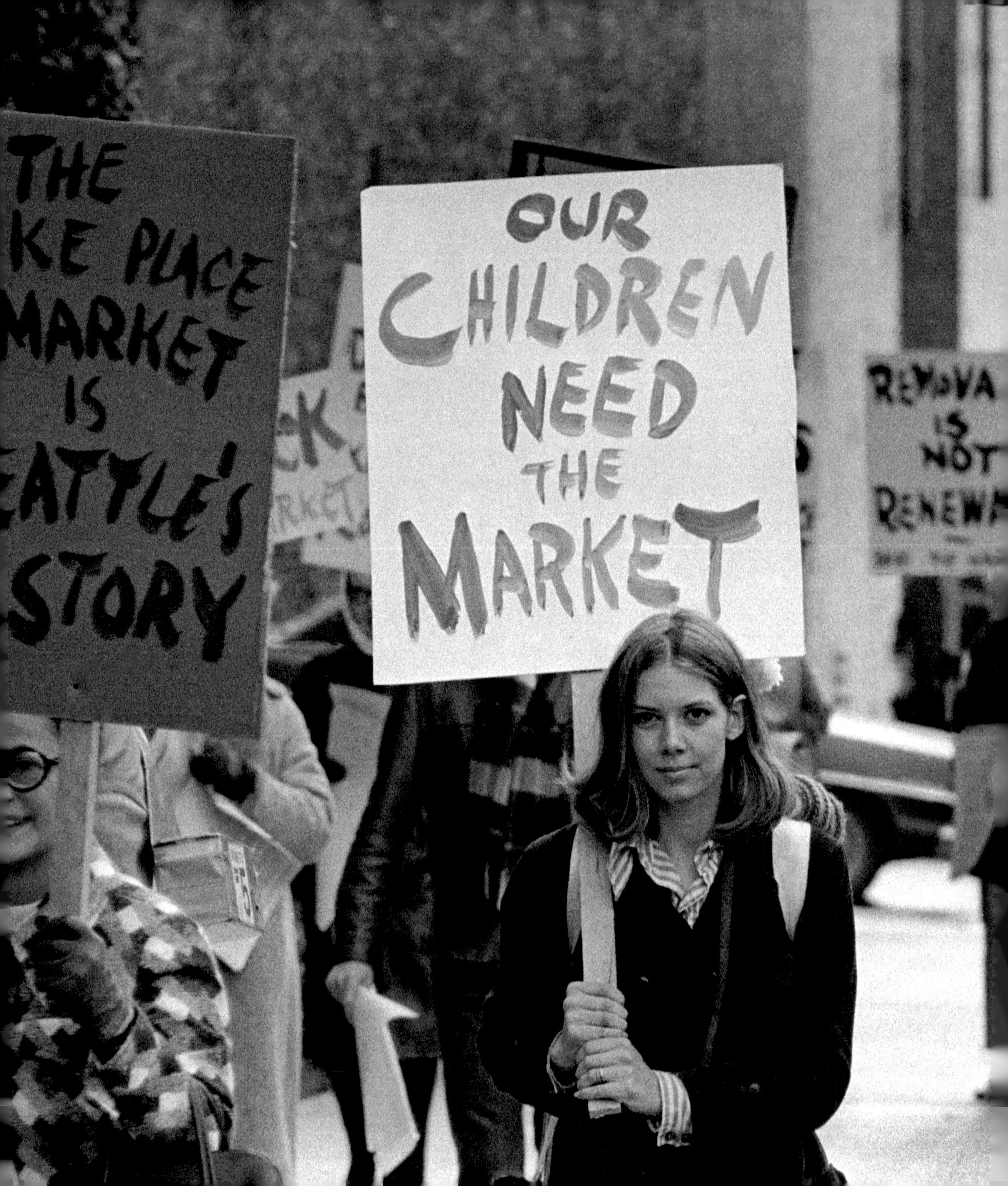
OUR CHILDREN NEED THE MARKET
THE
MARKET
IS
STORY

Chapter 3.

THE GREAT CORNUCOPIA

In the meat-and-potatoes era, fresh herbs like basil were hard to find in grocery stores. Home economics specialists—among them "King's Queen" Bea Donovan of KING-TV fame; her newspaper cohort, the pseudonymous Dorothy Neighbors at the *Seattle Times*; and Prudence Penny at the *Seattle P-I*—provided recipes touting frozen foods and canned soups. Seattleites, meanwhile, had a hint even then of what a critic called the "great cornucopia" near their doors.

An immigrant from Tuscany, University of Washington English professor Angelo Pellegrini spread the then-prophetic idea that the best meals come from carefully selected plants picked fresh from the garden. Quality food was an integral part of Pellegrini's life, a passion he shared with local friends and then with the nation. His books influenced modern leaders such as Ruth Reichl and Alice Waters.

Pellegrini baked bread in an outdoor oven he built himself, foraged mushrooms in the woods, pressed grapes for his own Cabernet, and tended an intensively planted vegetable plot at his home in View Ridge. His ideas harked to his Italian past and looked to the future, recommending Americans expand their palates to include dandelion greens and sweetbreads.

Even if aficionados heard the message promoting local goods, the city's main commercial option for getting them was in danger.

LEFT One of the few historically preserved farms in the city, Marra Farm is a four-acre oasis in the South Park neighborhood whose programs include community gardens, harvesting produce for local food banks, and educational projects. In this 2005 photo, Najah Nuth, a fourth grader at nearby Concord Elementary School, laughingly nibbles on an organic leek.

PREVIOUS PAGE Victor Steinbrueck and other demonstrators march in a successful campaign in 1971 to "Save the Market" from demolition. Supporter and celebrated Northwest artist Mark Tobey said he would never want to return to the city if the Market was demolished, calling it the "heart of Seattle."

Pike Place Market had already been diminished by the wartime years; just fifty-three stall leases remained in 1949. Its influence was frayed even further by the rise of supermarkets and suburbs and a loss of farmland.

In 1963, fearing blight, city lawmakers and the business-led Central Association proposed what they called an urban renewal for the Market. Opponents called it a death knell. The historic spot with its "million-dollar view" would be razed. In its place would rise three thousand parking places, a new hotel, and high-rise apartments. It would no longer be, as one resident was quoted at a public meeting, "the kind of place where little people come and shop for lettuce."[20]

Preservationists rallied. Architect Fred Bassetti branded the Market "an honest place in a phony time." Victor Steinbrueck, co-chair of the Friends of the Market committee, called it a "living ecosystem." Supporters gathered signatures to put an initiative on the ballot, creating a seven-acre historic district and establishing a commission to preserve and restore the Market.

On November 2, 1971, the preservationists won, 76,369 to 53,264. The Pike Place Market Preservation and Development Authority was formed in 1973, serving eventually as landlords and leasers. Generous federal restoration funds flowed in, aided by Senator Warren G. Magnuson. Sagging buildings were rebuilt to code, and appearances were refreshed.

In the process, the Market won an impregnable spot in the city's heart. It has faced, and won, more battles over the years: it's as unlikely now to imagine tearing the Market down as it would be to wreck the Space Needle.

Independent of the Market's struggles, a troubled Seattle was looking for ways to get food to the people. A plummeting economy, the national back-to-the-land movement, and a critical mass of idealists were fueling a full-fledged sustainable food movement. A municipal government willing to work with environmental activists provided crucial boosts along the way.

There were isolated projects, like the 1971 community gardens promoted

UPPER Henry and Phil Gai, pictured here in 1978, ran busy Gai's Bakery, at one time the top specialty bakery in the state. Their father Giglio Gai, an immigrant from Italy, founded it in 1931 as New Home Bakery, initially serving Italian truck farmers hungry for a taste of the old country. In the Depression era, Henry once told a reporter they would take produce, chickens, and rabbits from the farmers in lieu of cash.

LOWER "Prudence Penny" was a persona created by the Hearst newspapers to provide recipes and dispense advice to homemakers. Frances Martin, pictured here in 1938, was the second person to fill the Prudence Penny role at the *Seattle Post-Intelligencer* newspaper.

RIGHT Angelo Pellegrini made almost 130 gallons of wine each year with grapes from his friend Robert Mondavi's orchards, giving much of it away. Calling Pellegrini the "Father of Sustainability," today a group of Seattle food luminaries runs a foundation honoring those who follow in his footsteps—or garden trellises—furthering the cause of what he called the "Good Life."

in the Yesler-Atlantic Neighborhood Improvement Project, meant to revitalize the predominately African American neighborhood. Then there were projects that mushroomed: in the Ravenna neighborhood, UW graduate student Darlyn Rundberg lived near the three-acre Picardo farm, one of the last remnants of what had been a network of truck farms before the rise of supermarkets. Rainie Picardo allowed Rundberg and neighbors to garden parts of the rich farmland after he retired in the late 1960s. Then, unable to pay the $636 tax bill, he planned to sell.

Rundberg asked Seattle's city council to preserve Picardo's land for public gardening, hoping in part to teach schoolchildren to grow food and provide vegetables for families in need.

She scored help in two important areas: a receptive city council and allies among fellow members of the Puget Consumers Co-op (PCC). The co-op had incorporated in 1961 as a food-buying club for fifteen local families, run out of founder John Affolter's basement. Expanding fast into a storefront focusing on natural foods, it became not only an important marketplace but also a force in food politics.

ABOVE Rainie Picardo, who farmed three acres in north Seattle for more than forty years, once told a reporter he oversaw "some wonderful growing soil, some of the best in the city." That's still true, thanks to the P-Patch program founded after Picardo retired and the farm was in danger of being sold for development. It was the foundation of what's become a hugely popular community gardening program.

PCC managed the gardens. The city agreed to pay taxes on the land for two years. No chemical pesticides or fertilizers were allowed. The city purchased the property in 1973, soon after approving a citywide P-Patch program. At one point the program was the largest community garden organization in the country; it now includes eighty-eight gardens run by the Department of Neighborhoods, with a push toward providing equal access to lower-income neighborhoods and ethnically diverse communities.

The poor economy that helped spur the sustainable food movement also prompted the founding of Northwest Harvest, a hunger-fighting organization that today provides more than two million monthly meals statewide. In its early days it was the Ecumenical Metropolitan Ministry, created in 1967 by church leaders who decided fighting hunger would be the focus of their efforts to ease Seattle's unrest.

The Boeing bust of the early '70s, catastrophic aerospace layoffs in a one-industry town, showed leaders their mission had no short-term fix. Hunger, once seen as an issue of the poor and homeless, was revealed as mainstream.

Northwest Harvest established its fundamentals early: fresh, free, nutritious food to those in need, striving for "dignity and honor" for clients. Seeing how other programs failed when government grants were cut, they rely on their own fund-raising. They pioneered ways to offer fruits and vegetables to their clients. They seek out culturally appropriate ingredients and healthful meals otherwise too expensive for clients to find. Thousands of volunteers have pitched in from the beginning: growers, truckers and landlords, sorters and packers.

"The value we bring is because of people who care, and have made us what we are," said Director of Procurement Mike Regis.

Working in parallel and sometimes overlapping ways with those efforts was Seattle Tilth, now with a permanent home and urban agriculture

ABOVE Now the country's largest consumer-owned food co-op, PCC began in 1953 as a small buying club and then advanced to a humble Madrona storefront, moving to Ravenna in 1969. The Ravenna shop, pictured here, had handwritten bulk bin labels. The co-op has led food-politics issues such as banning all products with high-fructose corn syrup and carrying only fair-trade chocolates. What is now Central Co-op on Capitol Hill was formed when original members split off from PCC.

LEFT Mark Musick, pictured here at Pragtree Farm in Arlington, where he helped found the Tilth Association. Musick has spent decades supporting organic and sustainable agriculture in the region, including developing the now-ubiquitous "Seattle Salad" of wild greens and edible flowers such as fava bean blossoms.

center at the Good Shepherd Center in Wallingford. Envisioned "to support and promote biologically sound and socially equitable agriculture in the Pacific Northwest,"[21] Tilth's roots also came in the early '70s, when community organizer (and founding member) Mark Musick helped organize a 1973 Spokane symposium with an inspiring speech by poet and activist Wendell Berry.

Musick remembered Berry's galvanizing warning that we could not allow another generation to pass without preserving strong agricultural communities. And if we lost them, Berry concluded, "we will not only invoke calamity, we will deserve it."

ABOVE Long lines regularly form outside the Cherry Street Food Bank, run by Northwest Harvest. The late Ruth Velozo, the longtime director, is pictured here greeting a client in 2001 on her last day of work.

Brothers **Erling** and **Norman Nilson** helped popularize buttery fillets of smoked salmon to a nation unfamiliar with much beyond lox. The Nilsons, members of an Alaska-based fishing family, moved to Ballard in 1950, where their Port Chatham seafood company began producing Portlock smoked salmon. Writer **Roger Downey** credits Julia Child, who tasted it while in Seattle, with spreading its fame.[22]

By 1964 there were enough foragers in the region to support a Puget Sound Mycological Society, still flourishing today, organized by architect **Ben Woo** and future governor **Dixy Lee Ray**, among others. Through group expeditions and an annual festival, the organization helps newcomers divine where to find hidden morels or how to tell a mycological lobster from a hedgehog.

Historian Jeffrey Sanders wrote of the pivotal figure at Seattle Tilth and in local community gardening, **Carl Woestendiek** (Woestwind), who came to Seattle in 1973 because of the city's strong community of like-minded people and thriving counterculture scene.

Sunset magazine's first-ever pesto recipe came from Angelo Pellegrini in 1946. Less a recipe than a loosely written narrative, it was the first time many readers had heard of the now-ubiquitous preparation. The version below is from his classic book, *The Unprejudiced Palate*.

Angelo Pellegrini's Pasta al Burro and Pasta al Pesto

Serves 6

The recipe for pasta al burro is exceedingly simple. While the pasta is draining, melt a third of a pound of butter (for six portions) in a large kettle. Keep it over a slow fire, and toss the pasta in it briskly until the butter is evenly distributed. During the tossing, throw in three or four spoonfuls of cheese. Add, if you like, some minced parsley. Serve very hot with plenty of cheese over each serving.

For pasta al pesto, proceed as above, adding to the melted butter the following herb sauce: for a pound and a half of pasta, mince four cloves of garlic and enough fresh basil to fill a cup. The traditional method is to reduce them to a paste in a mortar and pestle, with the addition of small quantities of olive oil as needed. I have never used these implements, but I have achieved, I am sure, the same results with a sharp, heavy, straight-edged knife. A bit of patience and a little time are required, for the mincing must be thorough.

Chapter 4.

A GOURMET CITY

As people were taking some opportunities to return to the land, their palates were becoming more polished.

The first application approved by the new Pike Place Market PDA, in 1972, went to Shirley Collins to found cookware shop Sur La Table. Before Collins, the "culinary queen"[23] who loved fresh foods and fine cooking, cooks couldn't even buy a pastry bag in Seattle.

The former thrift store spot the Market preservationist found was small and dilapidated, but was the right place at the right time—particularly when gourmet cooking became a national trend. Collins's supplies and staff made it a cook's mecca, noted by culinarians like Julia Child as a rare source for new Cuisinart appliances. Now, under different ownership, it's the flagship of a national chain.

As home cooks became more adventurous, Seattle restaurateurs also shifted.

For decades, corporate restaurant chains with local founders had been the norm in Seattle. Many survive today, such as Restaurants Unlimited, with its waterfront Palisade (its original owners also cooked up Cinnabon, calling on local baker Jerilyn Brusseau to develop the nationally nibbled cinnamon roll).

Then came the individuals. Gerry Kingen obtained a liquor license when he was just legally old enough to drink, but was already an experienced restaurant owner. In 1969 he bought the first Red Robin restaurant, then a tavern. He reimagined it as a gourmet hamburger business, and the niche he discovered turned into a national franchise.

LEFT François Kissel (pictured here in 1981) and wife Julia were known for fresh ingredients and French flair at their Brasserie Pittsbourg in Pioneer Square. Lunches at the Brasserie were an institution in Seattle, wrote reviewer David Brewster, where "the aspiring young lawyers, government workers, journalists, and architects put in weekly appearances and busily scribble on the butcher paper, plotting the next bold maneuver to save the city."

A new wave swept the city when Julia and Francois Kissel transformed the venerable Pittsburg Lunch into Brasserie Pittsbourg in 1969. The French menu, sometimes prepared with ingredients from Pike Place Market, was credited with sparking new life in Pioneer Square.

Given the flagging economy, it might have seemed an odd time for a restaurant renaissance, yet food provided an opportunity for job seekers who didn't want to leave their beloved hometown. Restaurants were perhaps the best example, wrote historian Roger Sale, of a new consumer culture where it seemed everyone laid off from Boeing wanted to turn a lathe or cook an omelet. Young workers and female entrepreneurs entered the field, attracted by small-scale projects that weren't beholden to banks. "Cheeses, wines and coffees Seattle had never heard of became available,"[24] Sale wrote. Possibly, he presciently suggested in 1976, this rush of activity could push the city into culinary greatness.

Around that time, what had long been Rosand's Seafood Cafe, serving fishermen next to Ray Lichtenberger's boat rental and bait shop, was sold to new investors. The home-style fish-and-chips counter was refurbished and re-envisioned as a dining destination to match the scenic water views. It's maintained a focus on fresh seafood, and claims to be the first (in 1976) to get a license to buy fish directly from fishermen. A preparation of sake kasu black cod became popularized at Ray's in the 1980s as a dish almost synonymous with Seattle.

Almost.

Seattle's population encompassed many immigrant and ethnic groups, yet no one dish ever seemed to define the city the way that Philly has its cheesesteak and Maryland its crab cakes. The area has deep Scandinavian roots, yet its remaining eateries are considered more cultural hallmarks than city ones. Its Native American foods aren't widely available to the general public, though salmon bakes and stories are accessed through the tourist-friendly Tillicum Village on Blake Island, which opened in time for the Seattle World's Fair in 1962. Our

ABOVE In 1969, a twentysomething Gerry Kingen bought the Red Robin Tavern (pictured here in 1973), a student hangout at the south end of the University Bridge, reimagining it as a gourmet hamburger business and then a North American franchise. Kingen's many other Seattle restaurants over the decades include the Salty's chain of waterfront seafood restaurants.

OPPOSITE Ray's Boathouse remained a casual, home-style fish-and-chips stop for years, the site of events like this 1941 salmon derby. The food and decor eventually rose to meet the building's super-scenic views. In 1973 it was sold to new investors and rebuilt into a fine-dining destination.

UPPER The season's first shipment of Copper River king salmon being carried off the plane from Alaska to Seattle in 2013. The rich, fat-bellied fish were mainly shunted to canneries before tastemaker Jon Rowley popularized them as a delicacy in 1983.

LOWER At Le Gourmand, opened in 1985, Bruce Naftaly (pictured with wife and pastry chef Sara Naftaly) was called "The Godfather of Northwest Cuisine," an early champion of local producers and ingredients. He even grew his own poppies to harvest the seeds for his house-made crackers. After twenty-seven years, the couple closed their Ballard restaurant. Sara now owns Amandine on Capitol Hill, fulfilling her own dream of having a bakery, while Bruce teaches cooking classes.

seafood is iconic as an ingredient rather than a preparation; there's no single Seattle clam chowder, for instance, to compare with the clear-cut Boston version (though Seattle's well-known chowderman Duke Moscrip may beg to differ). Vietnamese pho noodle soup became a staple after an influx of immigrants moved to the area, yet no one would call any of these a Seattle signature.

Seattle Weekly critic Jonathan Kauffman made a scholarly case for teriyaki as Seattle's most distinctive dish. He credited Toshi's Teriyaki Restaurant, opened in 1976 by Toshihiro Kasahara, as the genesis of the ubiquitous businesses. Kasahara invented the then-unusual step of using sugar in his sauce, and presented teriyaki as an inexpensive and spare meal, serving sweetly marinated grilled meats with a scoop of white rice and a cabbage salad. Almost 2 percent of restaurants in King County have "teriyaki" in the name, according to Public Health Seattle–King County, with even more serving it at the counter.

If we didn't have one quintessential Seattle food, at least an overall style was becoming clear. By the 1980s, when chef Tamara Murphy moved to town, she saw the Seattle signature: we valued fresh local products and supported chefs who took advantage of them.

Bruce Naftaly opened Le Gourmand in 1985, using local ingredients in French-inspired cuisine—the sort of place where pioneering cheesemaker Sally Jackson would drive up in a station wagon with a cooler of artisan goods to sell.

Even supermarkets broadened their offerings. The upscale Larry's Market chain, assisted by Mark Musick, offered pre-made deli dishes, fine wines, and the "Seattle salad," believed to be the first packaged spring greens mix. Metropolitan Markets worked with local farmers and merchants; PCC expanded its number of stores and formed a nonprofit trust in 1999 to preserve organic farmland. Charlie's Produce, created in 1978, became the largest produce wholesaler on the West Coast, and included ingredients from regional farms in its orders.

Coffee Is King

Legendary columnist Emmett Watson wrote thirty years ago that it is the small things that make up a good city—and "one plus about Seattle, it seems to me, is that we have better coffee than almost any other city."[25]

Seattle had a history of major coffee roasteries, like Manning's, which was founded in 1908 in Pike Place Market. By the 1960s though, *Seattle Magazine* writer Gordon Bowker was driving to a specialty shop in Vancouver, BC, to buy good coffee beans. He decided Seattle needed a source of its own.

Bowker teamed up with Jerry Baldwin and Zev Siegel in 1971 to found their Starbucks "coffee, tea and spices" emporium at Pike Place Market. That first shop specialized in beans rather than brewed drinks, where bags of Sumatra went for a rich $1.75/pound and the proprietors warned customers that they roasted their beans dark.

Another six Starbucks opened over the next fifteen years, and they supplied hundreds of restaurants—quite a success, for a local business.

Rainy, cozy, international Seattle welcomed the coffeehouse culture, adding then-innovative offerings like Monorail Espresso. Billed as the city's first espresso cart, it was joined by hundreds of others, with espressos pulled even at gas stations and supermarkets. Seattle's reputation for quality European-style shots was cemented by restaurateur Kent Bakke, who imported high-end La Marzocco espresso machines from Italy. He eventually bought the company, at one time running a Ballard division that produced machines for Starbucks.

The real Starbucks explosion came with Howard Schultz, a onetime marketing manager for the company (and, as of 1987, owner) who believed the future was in prepared coffee rather than raw ingredients.

In some cases, Starbucks dominated its local competition. In 2003 it purchased Seattle's Best Coffee, a sizable chain that started out as the Wet Whisker, a Vashon Island ice-cream and coffee shop.

In other cases, competitors thrived by offering whatever Starbucks didn't. "Coffee prophet" David Schomer of Vivace started training countless aficionados in 1988 with exacting standards for selecting and grinding beans and pulling shots. He's been credited with developing latte art in the United States.

Employees of chains and independents alike branched into their own takes on the perfect brew. The list of names is as endless as the corner cafes.

UPPER RIGHT Coffee pioneer Jim Reynolds tastes a sample roast at Starbucks in 1983.

LOWER Scrupulous care was given to buying and blending the coffee. The aroma of the beans tantalized shoppers at Pike Place Market. We're not talking about Starbucks here, but Manning's, founded at the Market in 1908. By 1949, the date of this photo, the company had multiple restaurants around the city (the window pictured is on Third Avenue) in addition to the roastery.

It was a chicken or egg situation, Murphy recalls, remembering the revelation of seeing her first delicate spring salad greens picked fresh from Skagit Valley fields. As more locally produced products became available, "it drew more and more people to this area who wanted to be here, where it was happening. I think we were all sort of growing up together."[26]

The most definable turning point may have come in 1980 when former commercial fisherman Jon Rowley met up with restaurateur Robert Rosellini, son of Victor Rosellini. The meeting came at Rosellini's Other Place, a sensation where Robert sourced meat from a wild game farm and cooked it with outlandish fresh herbs—like tarragon. Edible nasturtium leaves graced the plates.

Rosellini had apprenticed in Europe and saw himself as "the self-appointed ambassador of flavor for the Northwest."[27] His own emissaries, such as Bruce Naftaly, soon spread across the city, with Rosellini alumni branching out to create their own landmark restaurants.

Fish was the only area where Rosellini's quest for quality stalled—until Rowley came for lunch one day and informed them that they could do better. The pair started the R&R Fish Company, working with Alaskan fishermen to improve the quality of fish in the Seattle market.

Quiet, watchful Rowley kept up his improvement quests in other areas over the years, with an enviable sense of taste and an uncanny gift for taste making. He reintroduced Olympia oysters, once ubiquitous in the area. Through berry-picking tours and shortcake bakes he popularized the craggy Shuksan strawberry, developed by Washington State University researchers but so fragile and fleeting that it tended to be sold for ice-cream production rather than retail. His most dramatic coup came in 1983 when he arranged for the run of rich, oily Copper River salmon—once designated for canneries or exported to Japan—to be flown directly to Seattle. The Copper River run became a national media sensation and an annual celebration of the seasons—a revelation for chefs as well as diners of a prize overlooked for years.

ABOVE Julia Child called Jon Rowley (left) "The Fish Missionary." They're pictured here on a 1983 fishing trip for her PBS series "Dinner at Julia's."

OPPOSITE Childhood friends Mick McHugh and Tim Firnstahl, pictured here in 1978, partnered in a long series of successful Seattle hangouts, including Jake O'Shaughnessey's and F. X. McRory's. Former *Seattle Times* restaurant critic John Hinterberger once wrote that "no one since Ivar Haglund had as much fun running a string of restaurants hereabouts as did Firnstahl and McHugh." When dissolving their forty-year partnership in 1988, they decided how to divvy the properties by tossing a coin from the top of the Space Needle.

Kasu black cod has a storied history in Seattle. A 1988 *New York Times* story credited Dick Yoshimura of Mutual Fish as pioneering the preparation at his market as far back as the 1940s. Shiro Kashiba claimed to be the first to serve it at a restaurant. Ray's Boathouse chef Wayne Ludvigsen told the paper he had tasted it at Shiro's Nikko restaurant and turned it into the Ray's version, still a classic.

Ray's Boathouse Black Cod in Sake Kasu

Serves 4; allow 48 hours for advance preparation

2 to 2½ pounds black cod fillet, skin on, cut into 4 serving pieces
⅓ cup kosher salt, more if needed
6 ounces (¾ cup) sake kasu paste
⅓ cup sugar
¾ cup water
Steamed choy sum
Sliced pickled ginger

Place black cod fillets skin side down in a shallow glass baking dish. Sprinkle a generous layer of salt over the fish, and then cover and refrigerate for 24 hours.

Rinse the salt from the fish and pat dry. Place fish skin side down in a clean dish.

Using an electric mixer, beat the kasu paste and sugar until smooth. Slowly add water and mix until incorporated. Pour the kasu mixture evenly over the fish, then cover and refrigerate for another 24 hours.

Prepare a charcoal or gas grill. When the grill is very hot, remove black cod from the marinade, allowing the excess to drip off. Grill fish until nicely browned and just cooked through, about 5 minutes per side. Transfer to individual plates. Serve with Sesame Rice Cakes, Wasabi Emulsion, steamed choy sum, and pickled ginger.

Gwen Bassetti was mother of the bread revolution that made Seattle a prime place to find an artisan loaf. In 1972, Bassetti and two partners opened a sandwich and pastry shop in Pioneer Square. The shop later became the redeveloped Grand Central Bakery featuring rustic Como bread baked in a hearth oven.

David Brewster provided the most telltale sign of a new golden restaurant age of restaurant dining in 1972, according to historian Roger Sale, when Brewster began publishing a monthly Gourmet's Notebook commentary on food and restaurants. Brewster later became founding editor of *Seattle Weekly* and the Best Places series of guidebooks.

Peter Cipra, Seattle's "dean of fine dining" in the 1970s and '80s, influenced future restaurateurs with his classical European restaurant, Labuznik.

Handmade pasta, anyone? Long before anyone knew the names **Ethan Stowell** and **Holly Smith**, the words "authentic" and "Italian" were linked to figures like **Luciano Bardinelli**, who opened Settebello in 1982, finding that Seattle reminded him of his Italian hometown. The same year saw the opening of Saleh al Lago, where owner **Saleh Joudeh** catered to the city's movers and shakers for seventeen years. **Carmine Smeraldo** followed with his fine-dining mecca, Il Terrazzo Carmine, in 1984, still run by his wife and children.

SESAME RICE CAKES

1 cup Japanese short-grain rice
1¼ cups water
2 teaspoons seasoned rice wine vinegar
1 tablespoon white sesame seeds
1 tablespoon dark sesame seeds
3 tablespoons canola oil

Place rice and water in a 2-quart saucepan and bring to a boil. Continue boiling for 1 minute, then cover pan and reduce heat to low. Simmer on low for 20 minutes. Remove from heat and stir in vinegar. Line the bottom of a 6-by-6-inch baking pan with parchment or waxed paper. Using a rubber spatula, transfer rice to the pan. Spread the rice out evenly and pack down tightly to about ¾ to 1 inch deep. Cool rice in the refrigerator.

While the rice is cooking, lightly toast the white and dark sesame seeds in a nonstick pan over medium-high heat. Constantly stir or toss seeds until the white seeds start to become golden, 3 to 4 minutes. Remove from heat and cool.

Preheat oven to 350 degrees F.

When the rice has cooled, carefully invert the baking pan onto a clean, flat surface. Peel parchment paper from the rice. Using a 3-inch round cookie cutter, cut into 4 cakes. You can also cut into 4 squares or other shapes, as desired. Sprinkle cakes evenly with sesame seeds and pat lightly. In an ovenproof nonstick pan, heat canola oil over medium-high heat. Place the cakes seed side down in pan, and sear until lightly browned, about 2 minutes. Turn the cakes over and bake for 3 to 4 minutes, or until heated through. Serve immediately.

WASABI EMULSION
Yields 1 cup

10 tablespoons unsalted butter
3 large egg yolks
2 teaspoons pickled ginger
1½ tablespoons wasabi paste
1 tablespoon rice wine vinegar
2 tablespoons warm water
Kosher salt

Melt butter in a 1-quart saucepan over medium heat, being careful not to burn it. Meanwhile, combine egg yolks, ginger, wasabi paste, vinegar, and water in a blender. With the blender running, slowly drizzle in the warm butter. Blend until emulsified. Season with salt to taste. Serve immediately.

Chapter 5.

A GENEROUS GEOGRAPHY

By the 1980s, Seattle's trademark industry was just starting its shift from aerospace to computer technology. It was also on the cusp of a culinary shift, with the arrival of Tom Douglas.

Cooking at Cafe Sport in 1984, the Delaware native began to make his name—and the first tracings of what would become "Northwest cuisine." His devotion to seafood "opened a city's eyes to its own bounty,"[28] wrote reviewer Kathryn Robinson. He promoted a comfortably adventurous fusion-touched fare. He shopped (as he still does) at Mutual Fish, picking up ingredients and ideas from Dick and Harry Yoshimura.

Already a minor celebrity, he opened the Dahlia Lounge with wife Jackie Cross in 1989, borrowing money from Jackie's uncle when no bank would stake them. At first, business was slow—too slow. But the Seattle community didn't let Douglas fail: the Yoshimuras supplied him with fish for months without sending a bill; friend and restaurateur Kenny Raider fronted him money for payroll. On New Year's Eve, counting on a sold-out crowd, Douglas flew in lobsters for a luxurious entree. Snow fell in Seattle and the restaurant remained empty.

In what's become the defining tale of his tenure, Douglas took inspiration from the wonton soup at Saigon Restaurant in Pike Place Market, and turned his fifty extra lobsters into 150 batches of lobster pot stickers to be frozen for future nights. They won raves on a four-star *Seattle Times* review, and business boomed.

Douglas launched forward, becoming a businessman as much as a cook. A second and third and now fifteenth restaurant followed, in addition to a cooking school, spice rubs, and an eastern Washington farm run by Cross.

LEFT Revered for supplying fresh fish and expert advice, Dick Yoshimura (pictured here in 1984) founded the Mutual Fish Company in 1947, credited with the region's first live seafood tanks and other innovations. Son Harry Yoshimura runs the business now, still a favorite of chefs as well as home cooks.

Douglas kept no secrets about his success: he was obsessive about details and food quality, sensible about money, a big personality who enjoyed the challenge of new adventures. His greatest talent might have been wisely choosing the people he hired; graduates from "Tom Douglas University" have multiplied his mark across the region, including some of the city's most influential restaurateurs—Holly Smith of Cafe Juanita, John Sundstrom and J.M. Enos of Lark, and Babe Shepherd of Red Mill Burgers.

Even early on, Robinson wrote that Douglas's consistent balance between sophistication and intimacy "happens to echo the driving ethos of this town, which holds its striving worldliness ever in tension with its inward devotion to the comforts of home."

The city defined Douglas as a chef, but he helped define us in return.

The Pacific Rim influences and the local ingredients that had always been in Seattle's background became an integral part of its cuisine, thanks to Douglas and others.

Asian ingredients met mainstream customers early on at the 1962 World's Fair, where Uwajimaya opened a popular pop-up shop. Much later, Rick and Ann Yoder spent two years exploring Southeast Asia before opening Wild Ginger with chef Jeem Han Lock. The *New York Times* said the city was a "chef's Shangri-La" undergoing an ethnic food revolution With its satay and cocktail bars, it featured a generous geography of Asian cuisine, from Malaysian curry to Bangkok boar.

Shiro Kashiba moved Japanese fare from the International District into the city's mainstream. He ran the first sushi bar at Maneki and one at his own Nikko restaurant. He later opened Shiro's in Belltown and, in 2016, Sushi Kashiba in Pike Place Market.

The excitement didn't just come from new arrivals. Canlis, whose reputation was a bit stodgy, made a sharp turn toward new relevance.

UPPER People always ask Tom Douglas, pictured at his first business, the Dahlia Lounge, when he's going to stop opening more restaurants. With fifteen and counting in his adopted town, he says he's never done with new challenges.

LOWER Red Mill Burgers, lauded for flame-broiled patties and crisp onion rings, is co-owned by Babe Shepherd. It's one of the many customer favorites around Seattle owned by former employees of Tom Douglas.

Pete Knutson, a commercial fisherman, an activist, and an anthropology professor, established the Loki Fish Co. with his wife, **Hing Lau Ng**, in 1979. Knutson is known for his gillnet-caught fish, but also for fighting to preserve Fishermen's Terminal as a working harbor.

Local promoter **Alan Silverman** dreamed up the first annual Bite of Seattle at Green Lake in 1982. Meant to boost restaurants during a recessionary lull, the modest event moved to Seattle Center in 1986 and now boasts more than 450,000 visitors per year.

RIGHT This Uwajimaya outlet at the Seattle World's Fair in 1962 helped the company blossom, introducing Asian flavors to a broad audience. Author Knute Berger once wrote that the Fair and the opportunities it provided helped turn Seattle into a dining destination.

When Peter Canlis died in 1977, his son Chris, with wife Alice, took on the challenge of following in the showman's shoes. They added personal warmth to Canlis and spearheaded renovations, but by the 1990s calf's liver was still on the menu and entrees came with a choice of french fries or rice pilaf.

The couple brought in consultant Greg Atkinson, who was overseeing a small San Juan Island restaurant with a seasonal menu. Atkinson revitalized the menu and added adventure. Canlis diners could still tuck into a steak and the eponymous mint-flecked salad, but could also feast on creations that drew glamour shots in national magazines. A new generation of owners, Chris and Alice's sons, Brian and Mark, now make the business relevant for yet another generation of diners.

ABOVE Shiro Kashiba trained in Tokyo with venerated sushi chef Jiro Ono. After moving to Seattle in the 1960s, he helped introduce sushi to the city. Decades later, he's still preparing omakase meals for customers, now famed in his own right.

OPPOSITE A chef who once couldn't figure out how to keep his own knives sharp, Seattle chef Bob Kramer eventually became a master bladesmith. His hand-forged knives are both works of art and coveted tools; top chefs from Mario Batali to Thomas Keller treasure his knives.

There Is Nothing like Les Dames

Moving to Seattle in 1993, star chef Holly Smith remembers thinking she "was super lucky to be in a city where women were in charge."[29] Unlike the industry's typical male-dominated kitchens, Seattle's food stars are as likely to be women as men, from chocolatier Fran Bigelow to *Top Chef* alum Zoi Antonitsas.

Some credit Seattle's younger culture, far from the hierarchical European model. Some point to a handful of early breakout chefs who paved the way for others. But a consistent support for women since 1988 has been Les Dames d'Escoffier. Seattle's branch, composed of women who have achieved professional heights in the food and beverage world, is focused on raising scholarship funds for female culinary students and mentoring women in the profession.

"Getting into the food world, the culinary world, for women is not—still, to this day—not that easy," said Beverly Gruber, the organization's first president and one of sixteen founding members. Members worked in supermarket management, as cooking instructors, recipe developers, authors, chefs, restaurant owners, winemakers. Among other endeavors, they support scholarship endowments. The first scholarship recipient, Lisa Nakamura, used it to help leap from her job as a flight attendant to culinary school. After a series of high-profile jobs, she now operates her own Gnocchi Bar restaurant on Capitol Hill. In 2012, going full circle, she was invited to join Les Dames, supporting newcomers.

Lisa Nakamura

An entrepreneur with an early interest in organic food and socially responsible farming, **Jeff Fairhall**'s vegetarian Essential Sandwich helped promote the idea of nutritious to-go meals. His many other ventures included cofounding the Essential Baking Co.

"Eat it and beat it." That was the slogan of the tiny Beeliner Diner, opened in Wallingford in 1988 by **Jeremy Hardy** and **Peter Levy**. Under the name Chow Foods, the business partners were early kingpins of Seattle's food scene, opening new restaurant concepts in different neighborhoods long before the practice became common.

LEFT The University District Farmers Market was tiny when it opened in June of 1993; newspapers reported "a laid-back atmosphere" with customers browsing through dahlias and organic mizuna. Now it's regularly on lists of the country's best and most authentic farmers' markets, inspiring others with its commitment to local farmers and growers. Each farmers' market in the city seems to have its own personality, attracting a loyal neighborhood following.

Seattle had long been a place where workers created their own solutions to the problems they saw. That characteristic took on a new edge when Seattle cook Bob Kramer noticed that kitchen knives were never properly sharpened. He left the stove and became a knife sharpener specializing in restaurants. In 1997, he became a certified master bladesmith whose hand-forged knives command a years-long waiting list and are coveted by top chefs around the globe.

Another problem-solver took on a 1990s version of the 1970s struggle to preserve farmland and provide local produce.

Chris Curtis, a former ice-cream-shop owner in the University District and a former Volunteers in Service to America (VISTA) volunteer, believed a farmers' market could both revive a neighborhood and save a threatened way of life on the rapidly disappearing open lands around Seattle.

In 1993, she organized the University District Farmers Market. A municipal boost again proved invaluable to an idealist—as she raised donations and pledges of volunteer time, the city's Neighborhood Matching Fund granted nearly $3,000 to start the market. More than twenty years later it's a year-round powerhouse occupying two city blocks, where chefs and home cooks alike seek out boxes of pristine peaches and bags of wild spring nettles.

The organization's markets have expanded around the city. Other agencies are active too, such as the Seattle Farmers Market Association, which manages the lively Ballard market. They work hard to maintain their space amid soaring development and grapple with the challenge of making their goods accessible to a broader and lower-income audience. Together, they bridge the gap between growers and diners of all appetites.

Feasts of Good Fare

Chef David Lee created Common Meals in 1988 to provide nutritious food to homeless and low-income Seattleites. Before long, in give-a-man-a-fish fashion, the organization grew into the nonprofit FareStart, which runs a culinary training program for people who are homeless or otherwise in need. (Lee went on to found Field Roast, the vegan meat company.)

More than seven thousand trainees have gone through FareStart's course, which includes cooking at the organization's welcoming downtown restaurant, and more than 90 percent of graduates soon obtain a job in the industry. A Who's Who listing of the city's finest chefs rotate through FareStart's Guest Chef Nights, cooking a three-course dinner at a bargain price. The stars and servers are all volunteers; the students get enviable kitchen training, and the diners get a gourmet meal. It leaves a good taste in your mouth.

FareStart student.

What is a Seattle food? How about tender tips of Douglas fir?
One of Seattle's first celebrity chefs, Kathy Casey, infuses them
into gin to evoke a "truly local flavor."

Douglas Fir Sparkle

Makes 1 drink

1½ ounces Douglas Fir–Infused Gin (recipe follows)
¾ ounce white cranberry juice
¾ ounce fresh lemon juice
¾ ounce simple syrup*
Splash of brut champagne or sparkling wine
Garnish: tiny sprig of Douglas fir, fresh or frozen cranberry

Fill a cocktail shaker with ice. Measure in the infused gin, cranberry juice,
lemon juice, and simple syrup. Cap and shake vigorously. Strain into a martini
glass, and top with a splash of champagne. Garnish with a fir sprig, and float
a cranberry in the drink.

*To make simple syrup: combine 2 cups sugar and 2 cups water in a saucepan,
bring to a quick boil, then remove from heat. Cool. Store refrigerated for up
to 10 days. Makes about 3 cups.

DOUGLAS FIR–INFUSED GIN
Makes enough for about 16 drinks

If fresh Douglas fir is not available in your area, then you can substitute a
Douglas-fir tea bag, available online. If using the tea, add the contents of the
tea bag to the gin, infuse, and then strain the gin through a very fine strainer.

1 (5- to 6-inch) sprig fresh-picked Douglas fir branch, rinsed
1 bottle (750 mL) of gin

Put the fir branch into the gin bottle, cap, and let sit 24 hours. (Do not let it
infuse for more than 24 hours.) Remove the branch and discard. The infused
gin can be stored at room temperature for up to one year.

Chapter 6.

MODERN METHODS

The city gained global prominence in the 1990s and into the twenty-first century. Seattle was suddenly the place to be, whether for its thriving and innovative industries, grunge music, or natural beauty. Just as with previous booms, newcomers spurred on a better and more international dining scene flush with creative opportunities.

As cooking and dining out became national entertainment, the idea of Seattle cuisine became more easily defined by the use of local and wild ingredients—augmented by global influences, invigorated by modern techniques.

The influences forming that perception came from more than the kitchen. People like Greg Atkinson helped shape it with evocative essays and cookbooks on Northwest food, and the priorities he passed on to students at the Seattle Culinary Academy. Other teaching centers stressed a Northwest cuisine as well, from Bastyr University with its nutrition program to the influential Quillisascut farm school in eastern Washington. Importers like Ritrovo and purveyors like World Spice Merchants made it easy for chefs and home cooks to introduce new high-quality ingredients.

A growing, progressive population with disposable income allowed potentially far-out ideas to thrive.

Maria Hines, who got her Seattle start in the kitchen of the W Hotel, opened one of the nation's first certified organic restaurants, Tilth. Even with her considerable cooking talents, her quest for sustainable and delicious meals was a difficult balancing act that required piles of documentation and difficult-to-source ingredients. Farmers like those at Skagit River Ranch would raise animals specifically for her. National acclaim swiftly followed.

LEFT Jeremy Faber, who founded Foraged and Found Edibles with then-partner Christina Choi, supplies wild goods to most of the city's top restaurants. Pictured here harvesting a sizable cauliflower mushroom in 2007, Faber says that "habitat is key. Until you know your trees and plants, forget about finding mushrooms."

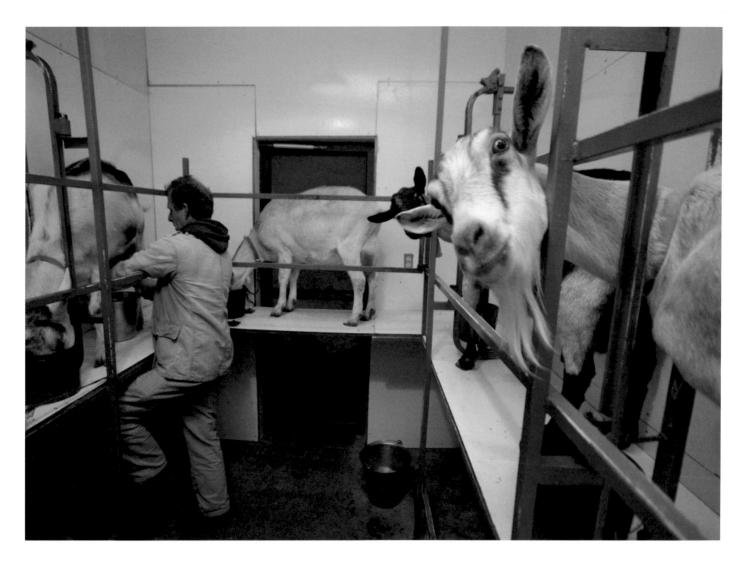

Among the sources for Hines's ingredients was Foraged and Found, established by a young chef couple, Jeremy Faber and Christina Choi, who had worked together at the Herbfarm. They supplied matsutakes, maple blossoms, and other treasures to restaurants and farmers' markets, bringing the mountains into city kitchens.

As Seattle continued to grow, another category of small suppliers came into their own.

Kurt Timmermeister, especially beloved by artists and writers for his Café Septieme in Belltown and then Capitol Hill, moved to a farm on Vashon Island where he offered secret underground dinners made with homegrown ingredients. He operated a dairy and later a farmstand cheese business, with an award-winning Camembert-style round named

ABOVE Quillisascut Farm is in eastern Washington, but the hands-on farm school that owners Rick and Lora Lea Misterly run has been a major influence on how Seattle chefs and culinary students support sustainable food.

after his first cow, Dinah. He went on to write well-received memoirs of farm life—and, in a recent full-circle move, to rely on his cows for an artisan ice-cream business in a hip new development back on Capitol Hill.

The city had tightly regulated street food in the 1980s, fearing a perception of "blight"[30] and restricting sales to only coffee, hot dogs, and popcorn. This led to the oddly regional "Seattle dog" slathered with cream cheese, but did little to help Seattle keep pace with the dynamic food truck pods springing up in Portland. The city finally tweaked the laws in 2011, and the area now boasts more than 125 trucks.

Rule-breaker Josh Henderson, who now runs the expansive Huxley Wallace Collective of restaurants, hit the city's tipping point when he started serving burgers with bacon jam out of a refitted Airstream in 2006. He remembers a crazy sense of community when he would pull his Skillet Street Food truck into a new stop and office workers would line up. When his credit card machine once broke, he issued IOUs—and says every last person returned to pay up.

In the 1970s, it had taken a bust for employees to focus on food businesses; in the 1990s, it took a boom. Programmers and tech experts at giant companies like Microsoft wanted to break out and start up; entrepreneurs were eager to invest in new ventures. Bellevue-based HomeGrocer.com tried to bring groceries to the front door—a little early, as it happened. The company, founded in 1997, was sold and then shuttered within a few years, a symbol of the excesses that led to the dot-com bust. Less than a decade later, though, Seattle's Amazon.com was spearheading a robust food delivery division where fresh milk (and cereal to pour it on) could be deposited at the front door with a few hours' notice.

Allrecipes.com, now one of the world's largest food sites, was cooked up in Seattle by grad students looking for a better way to organize their cookie recipes. It's sought out now for its community of forty million home cooks in twenty-four countries, providing user-rated recipes for any ingredient imaginable. The massive amounts of data allow the

UPPER An early consultant suggested HomeGrocer.com was an inconvenient way to buy groceries because customers would have to "fire up" the computer. Ultimately, consumers embraced online shopping, but it was too late for the trailblazing business.[31]

LOWER Maria Hines left a comfortable corporate restaurant job and risked everything to open Tilth, one of the country's first certified organic restaurants. Her inspired cooking as well as her exacting sourcing made it a success.

A Texas native who brought a rare taste of the South to Seattle, **Ezell Stephens** opened Ezell's Fried Chicken with childhood friend **Lewis Rudd** and other partners in 1984. The chicken and sweet potato pie, already loved by Garfield High School students and local celebrities alike, was made famous by Oprah Winfrey. Rudd's family still operates Ezell's; Stephens now runs his own Heaven Sent Fried Chicken chain.

Armandino Batali, father of celebrity chef **Mario Batali**, was a retired precision-minded Boeing engineer who studied traditional ways of meat curing from his Italian homeland. In Seattle he and wife **Marilyn** found a city—and a nation— ready to line up for Salumi sandwiches and Aunt Izzy's hand-rolled gnocchi. Daughter **Gina Batali** and her husband, **Brian D'Amato**, now own the business.

Thierry Rautureau, known as the "Chef in the Hat" for his trademark fedora, dazzled diners for twenty-five years with nine-course French meals at his Rover's restaurant. His approach changed along with the times, and Rautureau became a crowdsourcing pioneer in 2009 by raising money from customers to open his casual bistro, Luc, at a time when recession-scarred banks were reluctant to make loans. Loulay, Rautureau's latest venture, helped signify a revitalization of the downtown restaurant scene when he opened it in 2013. With pal Tom Douglas, Rautureau's also a major supporter of the hunger-fighting organization Food Lifeline.

Which food search terms are far more common in Seattle than in the rest of the United States? **Allrecipes.com** analyzed twelve months of data for MOHAI and found that five of the top-ten searches more common to Seattle included razor clams. Users inquired about trying them in fritters and chowders, and asked how to fry them. A cocktail recipe particularly sought by Seattleites was, no surprise, based on coffee (the sprinkle-topped "Coffee Nudge").

ABOVE In the early days of food message board eGullet, a user named "NathanM" once asked for recipe sources for a cooking technique known as sous vide. Finding none that met his standards, NathanM—a.k.a. former Microsoft Chief Technology Officer Nathan Myhrvold—founded his own cooking research laboratory and published groundbreaking cookbooks on modernist cuisine.

PREVIOUS Once food trucks got going in Seattle there wasn't much they didn't offer. Jesse Lee and Sheena Fuson serve sweet and savory stuffed hot cakes at their truck, My Sweet Lil Cakes.

company to spot shifting cooking patterns as fleeting as a city's cold-weather snap or as involved as tracking an esoteric ingredient's shift to the mainstream.

Star chef John Sundstrom worked with chef-turned-programmer Jared Stoneberg to develop what became a gorgeous crowdsourced cookbook paired with an interactive app. Innovative at the time for its funding as well as its contents, *Lark: Cooking Against the Grain* provided a view into recipes and ingredients that couldn't have been achieved even a few years earlier.

Rank-and-file tech staffers fueled many start-ups, but it took a former Microsoft tycoon to bring together food, science, and technology. When Nathan Myhrvold developed a fully equipped, fully staffed Cooking Lab division, it drew in some of the biggest talents in modernist cooking worldwide. His crew cavitated french fries in an ultrasound bath to obtain the crunchiest texture. They centrifuged peas. They spherified passion-fruit juice, eventually codifying their research into a six-volume set that was called the most important book in the culinary arts since the legendary Escoffier.

As his colleagues moved on from the lab, they further seeded the city with food visionaries. Work was tied to food for many Seattleites in ways unimaginable to the early salmon gutters or oyster shuckers.

Healthful and colorful, this is one of the most popular salads in the PCC deli case—and one of the longest lived. "I've been with PCC since the days of pencil and paper recipes, and nobody seems to recall the first batch," said deli merchandiser Leon Bloom. He thinks the mix of flavor and nutritional value is what made it such a hit: "You feel great after you eat it."

PCC Emerald City Salad

Serves 8 to 10, as a side dish

1 cup wild rice
½ cup olive oil
½ cup lemon juice
1 teaspoon minced garlic
Salt and pepper, to taste
½ bunch kale
½ bunch chard
½ red bell pepper, diced
½ yellow bell pepper, diced
½ fennel bulb, thinly sliced
1 bunch green onions, chopped
½ cup chopped parsley

Bring 3 cups salted water to a boil; add rice. Bring back to a boil, cover, and reduce heat to simmer. Cook until the water is absorbed, 60 to 65 minutes; remove from the heat and let cool.

Whisk together oil, lemon juice, garlic, salt and pepper. When rice is cool, toss with dressing.

Remove tough stems and ribs from greens, and chiffonade (cut into ribbons). Combine with peppers, fennel, green onions, and parsley. Just before serving, toss veggies with dressed rice.

Chapter 7

THE NEW BOOMTOWN

Despite its successes, the pressures of present-day Seattle seem as daunting as in the 1970s. Income inequity, rising land prices, food deserts, limited green space, and the aftereffects of the recession all underscore the need for more affordable access to good food.

As Seattle reaches new population heights, restaurants have become integral to its runaway cycle of expansion, an economic force as relevant as the fisheries and importers of the older city. Developers began working with high-profile restaurateurs to assure a sense of community and cachet in growing neighborhoods. At the same time, soaring housing costs put critical strains on workers, longer lines at food banks, tallies of more schoolchildren living in hunger. Fast-food workers walked off the job to successfully push for a hike in the minimum wage. Home cooks sought out organic and sustainably grown strawberries, while suppliers grappled with issues like fair treatment of the migrant workers picking them.

The array of food businesses grew broader, as when Jody Hall, an early executive at Starbucks, brought the gourmet cupcake craze to Seattle with her Cupcake Royale shops. Investing in employees as well as customers, she lobbied for health-care reform and baked rainbow cupcakes to support gay rights. After marijuana was legalized in Washington, she opened a separate business for pot-infused cookies and chocolates. She showed—yet again, for Seattle—that restaurateurs can become political forces as well as entrepreneurs.

Entrepreneurship itself was in no short supply, with people like Jerry Traunfeld. The chef spent seventeen years helping define Northwest cuisine with elaborate fixed-price dinners at the Herbfarm restaurant, then helped it evolve through his own more casual, globally influenced Poppy restaurant on Capitol Hill.

LEFT It seemed impossibly idealistic that the Beacon Food Forest could ever find enough volunteers to support the hard labor of work parties and land preparations— but the volunteers came, and they, along with their plantings, have thrived.

UPPER Leslie Mackie helped make Seattle a hotbed of fresh-baked artisan bread and fine pastries, opening Macrina Bakery in 1993 after years of working for Grand Central Bakery. Despite the company's enormous growth, Seattle restaurants and cafes still advertise the exact type of Macrina loaf or snack they serve.

LOWER After Pagliacci Pizza won *Seattle Weekly's* Best Pizza Award for more than twenty years, the newspaper gave the pizza chain a lifetime Golden Slice Award and ruled that it could no longer compete.

As the city has become bigger and wealthier, some small businesses have been forced out, yet others have been reborn. Large independent dairies have sharply declined, but small independent cheesemakers have thrived. Backers stepped in to buy and advance some Seattle classics, as when Matt Galvin and partners Pat McCarthy and Pat McDonald took over Pagliacci Pizza and DeLaurenti, and partnered with Macrina Bakery founder Leslie Mackie.

There was still room for surprises like 2238 Eastlake Avenue, a generic spot sandwiched between a Subway outlet and a teriyaki joint that wound up housing some of the defining chefs of modern Seattle. Susan Kaplan, original founder of the Boat Street Cafe, began the streak in 2002 when she opened scrumptious Sophie's Donuts. When Kaplan moved to a new Boat Street Cafe with cafe co-owner Renee Erickson, Matt Dillon took over the space—Erickson knew him through the monthly "Food Club" cook-togethers that the group of talented young chefs shared. Dillon put up a simple chalkboard menu and an inexpensive daily spread devoted to local and fresh ingredients. When he opened Sitka & Spruce, it was a twenty-seat strip-mall sensation of spring morels and wild greens, four-star dining in an informal setting.

Dillon eventually moved his flagship to Capitol Hill, and his old friend and colleague Christina Choi, cofounder of Foraged and Found edibles, inherited the Eastlake space. Choi turned it into homey Nettletown, dedicated to wild and foraged foods, Pacific and global influences, with shades of her own Swiss mother and Chinese father. One reviewer, before Choi's untimely death at age thirty-four, wrote that she was "allowing the woods to rule her menu." (The restaurant is now Blind Pig Bistro, featuring Northwest dining from chef Charles Walpole. As an early Blind Pig reviewer wrote, the space "sure has magic.") Erickson and Dillon went on to earn awards from the James Beard Foundation, known as the Oscars of the food world.

After long decades as an afterthought on the national scene, Seattle finally had a place at the table when glossy magazines and TV shows sought out innovative chefs or noteworthy trends.

A young chef named Ethan Stowell further laid the groundwork for that new prominence.

The son of Pacific Northwest Ballet founding artistic directors Kent Stowell and Francia Russell, Ethan cooked at the Ruins, a private supper club that became a training ground for many prominent city chefs. His elegant, critically celebrated Union restaurant closed after the dot-com bust, but Stowell was already off and running with Tavolàta, an upscale Italian restaurant. Then, a dizzying array of other projects: A sleek seafood bar. A salumeria. A ballpark concession menu. Pizzerias. He appealed not only to those seeking a downtown experience but also to the neighborhoods that had become mini enclaves. Stowell grew up in a Seattle restaurant scene where, as he recalled, there was no way to reach new heights except moving to a larger city. He first started opening new restaurants to give his talented staff members more ways to move ahead without moving out.[32]

The concept worked. Leaders like Erickson and Dillon and Maria Hines also moved from daily line cooks to big-picture overseers. And their own

UPPER Matt Dillon in 2007 at Sitka & Spruce, preparing the cauliflower mushroom that his friend Jeremy Faber foraged, pictured on page 62.

LOWER The culinary skills and creativity of Rachel Yang and husband Seif Chirchi make for an East-West cooking style that's indefinable except to say that it's their own—and, by extension, now the Northwest's.

employees, like former Dillon chef Edouardo Jordan, have branched out to become stars in their own rights.

Dillon, among his multiple other projects, followed up his national acclaim by leasing three out of four corners around Occidental Park. It was considered a daring location, where he established a smashing Mediterranean-influenced restaurant, a bakery-cafe, and a bar and private dining space.

Suddenly, Pioneer Square, not far from where those original Seattle settlers ate, was a hot spot. Some two dozen new restaurants and bars have followed Dillon's gamble, attracted by the beautiful old buildings and relatively lower rents, the sense of old Seattle, and the chance to revitalize—yet again—a historic district. More than a century later, it's still the place to eat.

So much of our history, it seems, involves such cases of moving forward even as we look back.

The line to dine is still long at Maneki, while Shiro Kashiba thrives at his new Pike Place Market restaurant. The Market itself is undergoing a new renaissance, with an expansion under way that was envisioned in the original Friends of the Market plans. Starbucks and Costco have become global giants rather than hometown heroes. Even Sea-Tac Airport, with

LEFT "Culture always inspired me," said chef Edouardo Jordan. Those include Southern and Caribbean influences from his childhood in Florida, African cuisine from his own studies, and fine-dining techniques from his jobs at prestigious restaurants during culinary school. After working for Matt Dillon in Seattle, he's won acclaim at his own restaurant, Salare, where he put parsley flowers on top of crab custards, accompanied duck with hedgehog mushrooms, and topped spiced beignets with chicory root custard. His goal: "I wanted to embrace my roots and find ways to create something different for this beautiful city that I call home."

RIGHT Renee Erickson credits her family with helping her make it as a restauranteur when she bought the Boat Street Cafe at age twenty-four. The assistance was literal—her dad built the patio, her brother bused tables, and her mom baked desserts. Even years later, when Erickson started her Boat Street Pickles business (pictured), Mom Shirlee helped her fill the jars. Her Walrus and the Carpenter oyster bar led one national magazine to dub her the chef who put Seattle on the map. It reminded her of the casual hangouts common in Europe but rare here—at least, rare since those nineteenth-century days on the Seattle waterfront.

🍳

Joe Whinney, cofounder of Theo Chocolate, the nation's only organic, fair-trade chocolate company, moved to Seattle to open the influential business in 2006 because he liked the city's entrepreneurial spirit. Theo is located in the historic Fremont building that once housed the Redhook Brewery.

ABOVE Christina Choi valued sustainability, community, and wonderful flavors. Even Japanese knotweed, a noxious weed, had a place on her menu.

Forest in the City

It sounded impossibly idealistic: a "food forest" on city-owned land, cared for by volunteers, open and free to anyone stopping by to harvest fruits and vegetables, nuts and herbs. The Beacon Food Forest was indeed "a dream design" when four students developed the plan as a project for a permaculture class. "It passed the course for us," said Glenn Herlihy. Then community members started asking if the design for a steeply sloped piece of land near Jefferson Park could actually become a reality.

Hundreds of people offered input. Outreach workers gathered advice from groups who might have been missed through language or cultural barriers. The Seattle Department of Neighborhoods P-Patch Community Gardening program became the umbrella organization, with some grants to excavate land and complete construction drawings. Then it was up to volunteers.

"We had no water, electricity, or anything out there at the time," said Herlihy, who, with fellow student Jacqueline Cramer, stayed with the project. "We just began holding work parties—2012 was our first one, September, and we saw 120 people show up, which was a shock to us. And we realized this project is about people and people management as well as land management." With the first 1.75-acre phase of the project now complete, plantings include annual tomatoes and kale as well as hazelnut trees, Vietnamese herbs, lemongrass stalks, and sweet summer plums. A particular goal was encouraging traditional foods from Native American communities, such as camas bulbs—after all, Herlihy noted, the area was originally "a forested garden of sorts" for local tribes.

Now that the project is literally bearing fruit, Herlihy said, "We teach how to harvest, how to harvest ethically . . . and so far that's been going great. Early critics said we were going to experience the 'tragedy of the commons'"—the classic economics scenario where individuals benefit themselves at the cost of the common good. That hasn't happened. "It's a complete reversal of the tragedy of the commons," Herlihy emphasized. "We are actually replenishing the commons, with good practices, and availability of land and yield and harvests to everyone."

a record forty-two million passengers in 2015, is showcasing homegrown eateries like Anthony's, Beecher's Handmade Cheese, and Kathy Casey's Dish D'Lish.

PCC and Uwajimaya groceries can now be delivered via Amazon. Meanwhile, some neighborhood farmers' markets are prospering enough to stay open year-round, with customers willing to step up for winter acorn squash as well as spring's fiddlehead ferns.

It's a context of abundance—and it makes our inability to pick a single defining Seattle dish feel liberating rather than lacking. We've come to see that our city's foods are both local and global, as exuberant as a public market and as intimate as a garden patch. We're as contemporary as a vegan food truck and as timelessly elegant as a plate of vermouth-poached prawns. From the view of Mount Rainier to the huckleberries foraged on its sunny slopes, from savory pho to sweet fair-trade chocolate, the food we eat is an integral part of the city we love.

ABOVE Shown here digging up tough winter root vegetables, Jerry Traunfeld is able to coax stunning flavors from fresh ingredients year-round.

Mark McConnell, a member of the Blackfeet tribe of Montana, noted a Seattle conundrum: despite the many members of different Native tribes living here, despite the traditional foods eaten at homes or at private gatherings, there were no public eateries serving Native American foods. He created the "Off the Rez" food truck with partner Cecilia Rikard and chef Donovan MacInnis, serving up sweet and savory fry breads with modern tweaks.

Molly Wizenberg, whose popular Orangette site was named the best food blog in the world by the (London) *Times* newspaper, was in the earliest wave of modern food bloggers, starting in 2004 as a diversion from her graduate work in anthropology. The blog led to two best-selling books and, with husband Brandon Pettit, whom she met through Orangette, three Seattle restaurants.

Rowley originally developed a version of this recipe for Anthony's restaurants, finessing it with a team that included then–executive chef Sally McArthur. When Silver Palate cofounder Sheila Lukins visited Seattle, she ate a version on a strawberry-picking trip with Rowley. She was so taken with it, she included it in her *U.S.A. Cookbook* as the best ever (for that riff, macerate just one-third of the berries, hand-tear another third, and slice the final third). Rowley recommends using Shuksan or Hood strawberries that have been picked the same day.

Jon Rowley's Strawberry Shortcake

Serves 6

FOR BISCUITS

2 cups all-purpose flour
1 tablespoon sugar
1 tablespoon Rumford baking powder (no aluminum phosphate)*
½ teaspoon salt
4 ounces (one stick) butter, chilled
1 cup milk
2 tablespoons cream

Preheat oven to 400 degrees F.
Grease a baking sheet.

Stir all the dry ingredients together in a large mixing bowl. Cut the stick of butter into small cubes, and work the cubes into the dry ingredients with your fingertips until the mixture resembles rough meal. Stir in the milk until the soft dough starts to pull away from the bowl.

Spoon the dough in six equal portions onto the baking sheet. Brush the tops lightly with cream. Bake for 15 minutes, or until golden brown. Cool completely on a wire rack.

*The aluminum phosphate used in most baking powders leaves a bitter, metallic aftertaste.

THE BERRIES

3 pints of ripe, local, June-bearing strawberries
2 to 4 tablespoons of sugar

Rinse and hull the berries. Set aside six small, whole berries for garnishing. Slice the berries into a bowl. Add 2 to 4 tablespoons of sugar, and let berries macerate for at least one hour.

WHIPPED CREAM

2 cups heavy cream, chilled
2 tablespoons sugar, or to taste

Using an electric mixer or wire whisk, whip the cream with sugar until it forms soft but slightly firm peaks.

ASSEMBLY

Slice a biscuit in half. Place the bottom half on a plate. Top with a layer of berries and their juice. Add a big spoonful of whipping cream. Cover with the top half of the biscuit. Then add another layer of berries and cream, in slightly smaller quantities than the first layer. Drizzle a tablespoon of juice over the whipped cream, and top with a small whole strawberry.

NOTES

1 "Chauncey Wright Stands at Head," *Seattle Daily Times*, 9/24/1911.

2 Advertisement, *Seattle Daily Times*, 10/11/1912.

3 Advertisement, *Seattle Daily Times*, 10/19/1917.

4 Theo Lawson, "Art Oberto's Boat Looking for Another Seafair Win," *Seattle Times*, 8/1/2013.

5 "Tomorrow to Be Birthday of Market," *Seattle Daily Times*, 8/16/1907.

6 Alice Shorett and Murray Morgan, *Soul of the City: The Pike Place Public Market*, Market Foundation in association with the University of Washington Press, p. 25.

7 Stuart Eskanazi, "Don't Call It Frango in Seattle," *Seattle Times*, 1/6/2005.

8 Bill Dietrich, "Ivar—The Celebrated 'Acres of Clams' Verse Is a Fitting Epitaph for the Long Life of a Generous Man," *Seattle Times*, 1/31/1985.

9 Hattie Graham Horrocks, *Restaurants of Seattle, 1853–1960*, 1960, p. 23.

10 William Speidel, *You Can't Eat Mount Rainier!*, Binford & Mort, 1955, p. 26.

11 Paul Dorpat, "The Dog House Restaurant Served Comfort on the Edge of Seattle's Aurora Avenue," *Seattle Times*, 9/13/2009.

12 Stuart Eskanazi, "Laurie Gulbransen Made Dog House Diners' Pet Eatery," *Seattle Times*, 11/7/2000.

13 Sheila Anne Feeney, "Dog House Keeps Patrons Coming Back," *Seattle Times*, 8/11/1981.

14 Michael Ko, "Seattle Restaurant Legend Victor Rosellini Dies at 87," *Seattle Times*, 1/11/2003.

15 *Seattle Post-Intelligencer*, 9/24/1950.

16 Speidel, p. 1.

17 Frank Chesley, HistoryLink.org Essay 8063, http://www.historylink.org/index.cfm?DisplayPage=output.cfm&file_id=8063.

18 Boyd Burchard, "Import Service to Gastronomes," *Seattle Times*, 11/26/1972.

19 Don Duncan, "Big Family Man: Restaurateur Has Spent 34 Years Making Seattleites Feel Welcome," *Seattle Times*, 8/5/1984.

20 Joyce Skaggs Brewster, "Market Wars," *Seattle Weekly*, 9/23–29/1981.

21 Mark Musick, "The History of the Tilth Movement," seattletilth.org, 2/12/2008.

22 Roger Downey, "Julia Child's Play," crosscut.com, 9/13/2013.

23 Nancy Bartley, "Seattle's Culinary Queen," *Seattle Times*, 2/24/1993.

24 Roger Sale, *Seattle Past to Present*, University of Washington Press, 1978, p. 240.

25 Emmett Watson, "You Can't Beat Seattle When It Comes to, Ahhh, Coffee Taste," *Seattle Times*, 2/4/1986.

26 Rebekah Denn interview notes.

27 Unpublished interview notes courtesy of Nancy Leson.

28 Kathryn Robinson, "It Just Gets Better," *Seattle Weekly*, 4/25/2001.

29 Providence Cicero, "Women Stars of Food & Wine? Seattle Has Them in Abundance," *Seattle Times*, 1/27/2014.

30 Seattle Street-Food Initiative, Director's Report, 2/15/2011, http://www.seattlegovtransportationdocs/stuse/SeattleStreetFoodInitiativeDirectorReport Feb162011.pdf.

31 "Virtual Groceries—Homegrocer.Com Courts Convenience-Hungry Shoppers to Turn Its Online Dream into Reality," *Seattle Times*, 11/29/98.

32 Rebekah Denn, "Everywhere Seattle's Chef-Owners Are Proudly Birthing New Places," *Seattle Post Intelligencer*, 9/11/2007.

REFERENCES

This catalog was researched with the benefit of MOHAI's archives and the wealth of resources at the Seattle Public Library, as well as Nancy Leson's generous access to her reporting files, menu collection, and original interviews. Books that were particularly helpful include:

Brewster, David. *The Best Places: The Gourmet Notebook Guide to the Pacific Northwest.* Seattle: Madrona Publishers, 1975.

Holden, Ronald. *Home Grown Seattle: 101 True Tales of Local Food & Drink.* CreateSpace, 2014.

Horrocks, Hattie Graham. *Restaurants of Seattle, 1853–1960.* 1960. (This original manuscript by a Seattle pioneer is available at Seattle Central Library.)

Hou, Jeffrey, Julie Johnson, and Laura Lawson. *Greening Cities, Growing Communities: Learning from Seattle's Urban Community Gardens.* Seattle: University of Washington Press, 2009.

Humphrey, Clark. *Vanishing Seattle.* Mount Pleasant, SC: Arcadia Publishing, 2006.

Sale, Roger. *Seattle: Past to Present.* Seattle: University of Washington Press, 1978.

Sanders, Jeffrey Craig. *Seattle and the Roots of Urban Sustainability: Inventing Ecotopia.* Pittsburgh, PA: University of Pittsburgh Press, 2010.

Shannon, Robin. *Seattle's Historic Restaurants.* Mount Pleasant, SC: Arcadia Publishing, 2008.

Shorett, Alice, and Murray Morgan. *Soul of the City: The Pike Place Public Market.* The Market Foundation in association with University of Washington Press, 2007.

LEFT Pike Place Market visitors can watch milk being transformed into cheese at Beecher's Handmade Cheese.

NEXT PAGE Sailors at unknown Seattle diner, circa 1940.